THIS PLANNER BELONGS TO:

_____

twenty 20

January
S	M	T	W	T	F	S
			1	2	3	4
5	6	7	8	9	10	11
12	13	14	15	16	17	18
19	20	21	22	23	24	25
26	27	28	29	30	31	

February
S	M	T	W	T	F	S
						1
2	3	4	5	6	7	8
9	10	11	12	13	14	15
16	17	18	19	20	21	22
23	24	25	26	27	28	29

March
S	M	T	W	T	F	S
1	2	3	4	5	6	7
8	9	10	11	12	13	14
15	16	17	18	19	20	21
22	23	24	25	26	27	28
29	30	31				

April
S	M	T	W	T	F	S
			1	2	3	4
5	6	7	8	9	10	11
12	13	14	15	16	17	18
19	20	21	22	23	24	25
26	27	28	29	30		

May
S	M	T	W	T	F	S
					1	2
3	4	5	6	7	8	9
10	11	12	13	14	15	16
17	18	19	20	21	22	23
24	25	26	27	28	29	30
31						

June
S	M	T	W	T	F	S
	1	2	3	4	5	6
7	8	9	10	11	12	13
14	15	16	17	18	19	20
21	22	23	24	25	26	27
28	29	30				

July
S	M	T	W	T	F	S
			1	2	3	4
5	6	7	8	9	10	11
12	13	14	15	16	17	18
19	20	21	22	23	24	25
26	27	28	29	30	31	

August
S	M	T	W	T	F	S
						1
2	3	4	5	6	7	8
9	10	11	12	13	14	15
16	17	18	19	20	21	22
23	24	25	26	27	28	29
30	31					

September
S	M	T	W	T	F	S
		1	2	3	4	5
6	7	8	9	10	11	12
13	14	15	16	17	18	19
20	21	22	23	24	25	26
27	28	29	30			

October
S	M	T	W	T	F	S
				1	2	3
4	5	6	7	8	9	10
11	12	13	14	15	16	17
18	19	20	21	22	23	24
25	26	27	28	29	30	31

November
S	M	T	W	T	F	S
1	2	3	4	5	6	7
8	9	10	11	12	13	14
15	16	17	18	19	20	21
22	23	24	25	26	27	28
29	30					

December
S	M	T	W	T	F	S
		1	2	3	4	5
6	7	8	9	10	11	12
13	14	15	16	17	18	19
20	21	22	23	24	25	26
27	28	29	30	31		

Year in Pixels

	J	F	M	A	M	J	J	A	S	O	N	D
1.												
2.												
3.												
4.												
5.												
6.												
7.												
8.												
9.												
10.												
11.												
12.												
13.												
14.												
15.												
16.												
17.												
18.												
19.												
20.												
21.												
22.												
23.												
24.												
25.												
26.												
27.												
28.												
29.												
30.												
31.												

Color Codes

Notes

January

2020

SUNDAY	MONDAY	TUESDAY	WEDNESDAY
			1
5	6	7	8
12	13	14	15
19	20	21	22
26	27	28	29

January  2020

THURSDAY	FRIDAY	SATURDAY	NOTES
2	3	4	○
			○
			○
			○
			○
9	10	11	○
			○
			○
			○
16	17	18	○
			○
			○
			○
			○
23	24	25	○
			○
			○
			○
			○
30	31		NOTES

February  2020

SUNDAY	MONDAY	TUESDAY	WEDNESDAY
2	3	4	5
9	10	11	12
16	17	18	19
23	24	25	26

February  2020

THURSDAY	FRIDAY	SATURDAY	NOTES
		1	○
			○
			○
			○
			○
6	7	8	○
			○
			○
			○
13	14	15	○
			○
			○
			○
			○
20	21	22	○
			○
			○
			○
			○
27	28	29	NOTES

March  2020

SUNDAY	MONDAY	TUESDAY	WEDNESDAY
1	2	3	4
8	9	10	11
15	16	17	18
22	23	24	25
29	30	31	

 # March
2020

THURSDAY	FRIDAY	SATURDAY	NOTES
5	6	7	○
			○
			○
			○
			○
12	13	14	○
			○
			○
			○
			○
19	20	21	○
			○
			○
			○
			○
26	27	28	○
			○
			○
			○
			○
			NOTES

April 2020

SUNDAY	MONDAY	TUESDAY	WEDNESDAY
			1
5	6	7	8
12	13	14	15
19	20	21	22
26	27	28	29

 April   2020

THURSDAY	FRIDAY	SATURDAY	NOTES
2	3	4	○
			○
			○
			○
			○
9	10	11	○
			○
			○
			○
16	17	18	○
			○
			○
			○
			○
23	24	25	○
			○
			○
			○
			○
30			NOTES

May

SUNDAY	MONDAY	TUESDAY	WEDNESDAY
3	4	5	6
10	11	12	13
17	18	19	20
24	25	26	27

May  2020

THURSDAY	FRIDAY	SATURDAY	NOTES
	1	2	○
			○
			○
			○
			○
7	8	9	○
			○
			○
			○
14	15	16	○
			○
			○
			○
			○
21	22	23	○
			○
			○
			○
			○
28	29	30	NOTES
		SUNDAY 31	

June  2020

SUNDAY	MONDAY	TUESDAY	WEDNESDAY
	1	2	3
7	8	9	10
14	15	16	17
21	22	23	24
28	29	30	

June  2020

THURSDAY	FRIDAY	SATURDAY	NOTES
4	5	6	○
			○
			○
			○
			○
11	12	13	○
			○
			○
			○
18	19	20	○
			○
			○
			○
			○
25	26	27	○
			○
			○
			○
			○
			NOTES

July

SUNDAY	MONDAY	TUESDAY	WEDNESDAY
			1
5	6	7	8
12	13	14	15
19	20	21	22
26	27	28	29

July

2020

THURSDAY	FRIDAY	SATURDAY	NOTES
2	3	4	○
			○
			○
			○
			○
9	10	11	○
			○
			○
			○
16	17	18	○
			○
			○
			○
			○
23	24	25	○
			○
			○
			○
			○
30	31		NOTES

August 2020

SUNDAY	MONDAY	TUESDAY	WEDNESDAY
2	3	4	5
9	10	11	12
16	17	18	19
23 / 30	24 / 31	25	26

August

THURSDAY	FRIDAY	SATURDAY	NOTES
		1	○
			○
			○
			○
			○
6	7	8	○
			○
			○
			○
13	14	15	○
			○
			○
			○
			○
20	21	22	NOTES
27	28	29	

September 2020

SUNDAY	MONDAY	TUESDAY	WEDNESDAY
		1	2
6	7	8	9
13	14	15	16
20	21	22	23
27	28	29	30

September

THURSDAY	FRIDAY	SATURDAY	NOTES
3	4	5	○
			○
			○
			○
			○
10	11	12	○
			○
			○
			○
17	18	19	○
			○
			○
			○
			○
24	25	26	○
			○
			○
			○
			○
			NOTES

October

SUNDAY	MONDAY	TUESDAY	WEDNESDAY
4	5	6	7
11	12	13	14
18	19	20	21
25	26	27	28

October  2020

THURSDAY	FRIDAY	SATURDAY	NOTES
1	2	3	○
			○
			○
			○
			○
8	9	10	○
			○
			○
			○
15	16	17	○
			○
			○
			○
			○
22	23	24	○
			○
			○
			○
			○
29	30	31	NOTES

 November 2020

SUNDAY	MONDAY	TUESDAY	WEDNESDAY
1	2	3	4
8	9	10	11
15	16	17	18
22	23	24	25
29	30		

November  2020

THURSDAY	FRIDAY	SATURDAY	NOTES
5	6	7	○
			○
			○
			○
			○
12	13	14	○
			○
			○
			○
			○
19	20	21	○
			○
			○
			○
			○
26	27	28	○
			○
			○
			○
			○
			NOTES

December  2020

SUNDAY	MONDAY	TUESDAY	WEDNESDAY
		1	2
6	7	8	9
13	14	15	16
20	21	22	23
27	28	29	30

December

THURSDAY	FRIDAY	SATURDAY	NOTES
3	4	5	○
			○
			○
			○
			○
10	11	12	○
			○
			○
			○
17	18	19	○
			○
			○
			○
			○
24	25	26	○
			○
			○
			○
			○
31			NOTES

December
2019

01 SUNDAY
- ○ _____
- ○ _____
- ○ _____
- ○ _____
- ○ _____
- ○ _____
- ○ _____
- ○ _____

02 MONDAY
- ○ _____
- ○ _____
- ○ _____
- ○ _____
- ○ _____
- ○ _____
- ○ _____
- ○ _____

03 TUESDAY
- ○ _____
- ○ _____
- ○ _____
- ○ _____
- ○ _____
- ○ _____
- ○ _____
- ○ _____

04 WEDNESDAY
- ○ _____
- ○ _____
- ○ _____
- ○ _____
- ○ _____

December
2019

05 THURSDAY

○ _____
○ _____
○ _____
○ _____
○ _____
○ _____
○ _____
○ _____

06 FRIDAY

○ _____
○ _____
○ _____
○ _____
○ _____
○ _____
○ _____
○ _____
○ _____

07 SATURDAY

○ _____
○ _____
○ _____
○ _____
○ _____
○ _____
○ _____
○ _____

08 SUNDAY

○ _____
○ _____
○ _____
○ _____
○ _____

09 MONDAY

○ _____
○ _____
○ _____
○ _____
○ _____
○ _____
○ _____
○ _____

10 TUESDAY

○ _____
○ _____
○ _____
○ _____
○ _____
○ _____
○ _____
○ _____

11 WEDNESDAY

○ _____
○ _____
○ _____
○ _____
○ _____
○ _____
○ _____
○ _____

12 THURSDAY

○ _____
○ _____
○ _____
○ _____
○ _____

December
2019

13 FRIDAY
○
○
○
○
○
○
○
○

14 SATURDAY
○
○
○
○
○
○
○
○

15 SUNDAY
○
○
○
○
○
○
○
○

16 MONDAY
○
○
○
○
○

17 TUESDAY

○ _____
○ _____
○ _____
○ _____
○ _____
○ _____
○ _____
○ _____

18 WEDNESDAY

○ _____
○ _____
○ _____
○ _____
○ _____
○ _____
○ _____
○ _____

19 THURSDAY

○ _____
○ _____
○ _____
○ _____
○ _____
○ _____
○ _____
○ _____

20 FRIDAY

○ _____
○ _____
○ _____
○ _____
○ _____

December
2019

21 SATURDAY
○
○
○
○
○
○
○
○

22 SUNDAY
○
○
○
○
○
○
○
○

23 MONDAY
○
○
○
○
○
○
○
○

24 TUESDAY
○
○
○
○
○

December
2019

25 WEDNESDAY

○ _____
○ _____
○ _____
○ _____
○ _____
○ _____
○ _____
○ _____

26 THURSDAY

○ _____
○ _____
○ _____
○ _____
○ _____
○ _____
○ _____
○ _____

27 FRIDAY

○ _____
○ _____
○ _____
○ _____
○ _____
○ _____
○ _____
○ _____

28 SATURDAY

○ _____
○ _____
○ _____
○ _____
○ _____

December
2019

29 SUNDAY
- ○
- ○
- ○
- ○
- ○
- ○
- ○
- ○

30 MONDAY
- ○
- ○
- ○
- ○
- ○
- ○
- ○
- ○

31 TUESDAY
- ○
- ○
- ○
- ○
- ○
- ○
- ○
- ○

NOTES

January
2020

01 WEDNESDAY
○ _____
○ _____
○ _____
○ _____
○ _____
○ _____
○ _____
○ _____

02 THURSDAY
○ _____
○ _____
○ _____
○ _____
○ _____
○ _____
○ _____
○ _____

03 FRIDAY
○ _____
○ _____
○ _____
○ _____
○ _____
○ _____
○ _____
○ _____

04 SATURDAY
○ _____
○ _____
○ _____
○ _____
○ _____

January
2020

05 SUNDAY

○ _____
○ _____
○ _____
○ _____
○ _____
○ _____
○ _____
○ _____

06 MONDAY

○ _____
○ _____
○ _____
○ _____
○ _____
○ _____
○ _____
○ _____

07 TUESDAY

○ _____
○ _____
○ _____
○ _____
○ _____
○ _____
○ _____
○ _____

08 WEDNESDAY

○ _____
○ _____
○ _____
○ _____
○ _____

09 THURSDAY

○ _____
○ _____
○ _____
○ _____
○ _____
○ _____
○ _____
○ _____

10 FRIDAY

○ _____
○ _____
○ _____
○ _____
○ _____
○ _____
○ _____
○ _____

11 SATURDAY

○ _____
○ _____
○ _____
○ _____
○ _____
○ _____
○ _____
○ _____

12 SUNDAY

○ _____
○ _____
○ _____
○ _____
○ _____

13 MONDAY

○
○
○
○
○
○
○
○

14 TUESDAY

○
○
○
○
○
○
○
○

15 WEDNESDAY

○
○
○
○
○
○
○
○

16 THURSDAY

○
○
○
○
○

17 FRIDAY

○ _____
○ _____
○ _____
○ _____
○ _____
○ _____
○ _____
○ _____

18 SATURDAY

○ _____
○ _____
○ _____
○ _____
○ _____
○ _____
○ _____
○ _____

19 SUNDAY

○ _____
○ _____
○ _____
○ _____
○ _____
○ _____
○ _____
○ _____

20 MONDAY

○ _____
○ _____
○ _____
○ _____
○ _____

21 TUESDAY

○ \
○ \
○ \
○ \
○ \
○ \
○ \
○

22 WEDNESDAY

○ \
○ \
○ \
○ \
○ \
○ \
○ \
○

23 THURSDAY

○ \
○ \
○ \
○ \
○ \
○ \
○ \
○

24 FRIDAY

○ \
○ \
○ \
○ \
○

25 SATURDAY
○ _____
○ _____
○ _____
○ _____
○ _____
○ _____
○ _____
○ _____

26 SUNDAY
○ _____
○ _____
○ _____
○ _____
○ _____
○ _____
○ _____
○ _____

27 MONDAY
○ _____
○ _____
○ _____
○ _____
○ _____
○ _____
○ _____
○ _____

28 TUESDAY
○ _____
○ _____
○ _____
○ _____
○ _____

January
2020

29 WEDNESDAY

○
○
○
○
○
○
○
○

30 THURSDAY

○
○
○
○
○
○
○
○

31 FRIDAY

○
○
○
○
○
○
○
○

NOTES

01 SATURDAY

02 SUNDAY

03 MONDAY

04 TUESDAY

February
2020

05 WEDNESDAY

○ _____
○ _____
○ _____
○ _____
○ _____
○ _____
○ _____
○ _____

06 THURSDAY

○ _____
○ _____
○ _____
○ _____
○ _____
○ _____
○ _____
○ _____

07 FRIDAY

○ _____
○ _____
○ _____
○ _____
○ _____
○ _____
○ _____
○ _____

08 SATURDAY

○ _____
○ _____
○ _____
○ _____
○ _____

February
2020

09 SUNDAY
○
○
○
○
○
○
○
○

10 MONDAY
○
○
○
○
○
○
○
○

11 TUESDAY
○
○
○
○
○
○
○
○

12 WEDNESDAY
○
○
○
○
○

February
2020

13 THURSDAY

○ _____
○ _____
○ _____
○ _____
○ _____
○ _____
○ _____
○ _____

14 FRIDAY

○ _____
○ _____
○ _____
○ _____
○ _____
○ _____
○ _____
○ _____

15 SATURDAY

○ _____
○ _____
○ _____
○ _____
○ _____
○ _____
○ _____
○ _____

16 SUNDAY

○ _____
○ _____
○ _____
○ _____
○ _____

17 MONDAY

○
○
○
○
○
○
○
○

18 TUESDAY

○
○
○
○
○
○
○
○

19 WEDNESDAY

○
○
○
○
○
○
○
○

20 THURSDAY

○
○
○
○
○

21 FRIDAY
○
○
○
○
○
○
○
○

22 SATURDAY
○
○
○
○
○
○
○
○

23 SUNDAY
○
○
○
○
○
○
○
○

24 MONDAY
○
○
○
○
○

February
2020

25 TUESDAY
○ _____
○ _____
○ _____
○ _____
○ _____
○ _____
○ _____
○ _____

26 WEDNESDAY
○ _____
○ _____
○ _____
○ _____
○ _____
○ _____
○ _____
○ _____

27 THURSDAY
○ _____
○ _____
○ _____
○ _____
○ _____
○ _____
○ _____
○ _____

28 FRIDAY
○ _____
○ _____
○ _____
○ _____
○ _____

29 SATURDAY

○ _____

○ _____

○ _____

○ _____

○ _____

○ _____

○ _____

○ _____

NOTES

01 SUNDAY

○ _____
○ _____
○ _____
○ _____
○ _____
○ _____
○ _____
○ _____

02 MONDAY

○ _____
○ _____
○ _____
○ _____
○ _____
○ _____
○ _____
○ _____

03 TUESDAY

○ _____
○ _____
○ _____
○ _____
○ _____
○ _____
○ _____
○ _____

04 WEDNESDAY

○ _____
○ _____
○ _____
○ _____
○ _____

March
2020

05 THURSDAY
○ _____
○ _____
○ _____
○ _____
○ _____
○ _____
○ _____
○ _____

06 FRIDAY
○ _____
○ _____
○ _____
○ _____
○ _____
○ _____
○ _____
○ _____

07 SATURDAY
○ _____
○ _____
○ _____
○ _____
○ _____
○ _____
○ _____
○ _____

08 SUNDAY
○ _____
○ _____
○ _____
○ _____
○ _____

March
2020

09 MONDAY
○ _____
○ _____
○ _____
○ _____
○ _____
○ _____
○ _____
○ _____

10 TUESDAY
○ _____
○ _____
○ _____
○ _____
○ _____
○ _____
○ _____
○ _____

11 WEDNESDAY
○ _____
○ _____
○ _____
○ _____
○ _____
○ _____
○ _____
○ _____

12 THURSDAY
○ _____
○ _____
○ _____
○ _____
○ _____

13 FRIDAY

○ _____
○ _____
○ _____
○ _____
○ _____
○ _____
○ _____
○ _____

14 SATURDAY

○ _____
○ _____
○ _____
○ _____
○ _____
○ _____
○ _____
○ _____

15 SUNDAY

○ _____
○ _____
○ _____
○ _____
○ _____
○ _____
○ _____
○ _____

16 MONDAY

○ _____
○ _____
○ _____
○ _____
○ _____

17 TUESDAY

○ _____
○ _____
○ _____
○ _____
○ _____
○ _____
○ _____
○ _____

18 WEDNESDAY

○ _____
○ _____
○ _____
○ _____
○ _____
○ _____
○ _____
○ _____

19 THURSDAY

○ _____
○ _____
○ _____
○ _____
○ _____
○ _____
○ _____
○ _____

20 FRIDAY

○ _____
○ _____
○ _____
○ _____
○ _____

21 SATURDAY
○
○
○
○
○
○
○

22 SUNDAY
○
○
○
○
○
○
○
○

23 MONDAY
○
○
○
○
○
○
○
○

24 TUESDAY
○
○
○
○
○

25 WEDNESDAY

○ _____
○ _____
○ _____
○ _____
○ _____
○ _____
○ _____
○ _____

26 THURSDAY

○ _____
○ _____
○ _____
○ _____
○ _____
○ _____
○ _____
○ _____

27 FRIDAY

○ _____
○ _____
○ _____
○ _____
○ _____
○ _____
○ _____
○ _____

28 SATURDAY

○ _____
○ _____
○ _____
○ _____
○ _____

March
2020

29 SUNDAY

○ _____
○ _____
○ _____
○ _____
○ _____
○ _____
○ _____
○ _____

30 MONDAY

○ _____
○ _____
○ _____
○ _____
○ _____
○ _____
○ _____
○ _____

31 TUESDAY

○ _____
○ _____
○ _____
○ _____
○ _____
○ _____
○ _____
○ _____

NOTES

_____
_____
_____
_____

April
2020

01 WEDNESDAY

○ _____
○ _____
○ _____
○ _____
○ _____
○ _____
○ _____
○ _____

02 THURSDAY

○ _____
○ _____
○ _____
○ _____
○ _____
○ _____
○ _____
○ _____

03 FRIDAY

○ _____
○ _____
○ _____
○ _____
○ _____
○ _____
○ _____
○ _____

04 SATURDAY

○ _____
○ _____
○ _____
○ _____
○ _____

April
2020

05 SUNDAY

○

○

○

○

○

○

○

○

06 MONDAY

○

○

○

○

○

○

○

○

07 TUESDAY

○

○

○

○

○

○

○

○

08 WEDNESDAY

○

○

○

○

○

09 THURSDAY

○
_____
○
_____
○
_____
○
_____
○
_____
○
_____
○
_____
○
_____

10 FRIDAY

○
_____
○
_____
○
_____
○
_____
○
_____
○
_____
○
_____
○
_____

11 SATURDAY

○
_____
○
_____
○
_____
○
_____
○
_____
○
_____
○
_____
○
_____

12 SUNDAY

○
_____
○
_____
○
_____
○
_____
○
_____

April
2020

13 MONDAY

14 TUESDAY

15 WEDNESDAY

16 THURSDAY

April
2020

17 FRIDAY

○
○
○
○
○
○
○
○

18 SATURDAY

○
○
○
○
○
○
○
○

19 SUNDAY

○
○
○
○
○
○
○
○

20 MONDAY

○
○
○
○
○

21 TUESDAY

○ _____
○ _____
○ _____
○ _____
○ _____
○ _____
○ _____
○ _____

22 WEDNESDAY

○ _____
○ _____
○ _____
○ _____
○ _____
○ _____
○ _____
○ _____
○ _____

23 THURSDAY

○ _____
○ _____
○ _____
○ _____
○ _____
○ _____
○ _____
○ _____

24 FRIDAY

○ _____
○ _____
○ _____
○ _____
○ _____

25 SATURDAY

○ _____
○ _____
○ _____
○ _____
○ _____
○ _____
○ _____
○ _____

26 SUNDAY

○ _____
○ _____
○ _____
○ _____
○ _____
○ _____
○ _____
○ _____

27 MONDAY

○ _____
○ _____
○ _____
○ _____
○ _____
○ _____
○ _____
○ _____

28 TUESDAY

○ _____
○ _____
○ _____
○ _____
○ _____

April
2020

29 WEDNESDAY

○ _____
○ _____
○ _____
○ _____
○ _____
○ _____
○ _____
○ _____

30 THURSDAY

○ _____
○ _____
○ _____
○ _____
○ _____
○ _____
○ _____
○ _____

NOTES

_____
_____
_____
_____
_____
_____
_____
_____
_____
_____
_____
_____
_____

May
2020

01 FRIDAY
- ○ _____
- ○ _____
- ○ _____
- ○ _____
- ○ _____
- ○ _____
- ○ _____
- ○ _____

02 SATURDAY
- ○ _____
- ○ _____
- ○ _____
- ○ _____
- ○ _____
- ○ _____
- ○ _____
- ○ _____

03 SUNDAY
- ○ _____
- ○ _____
- ○ _____
- ○ _____
- ○ _____
- ○ _____
- ○ _____
- ○ _____

04 MONDAY
- ○ _____
- ○ _____
- ○ _____
- ○ _____
- ○ _____

05 TUESDAY
○
○
○
○
○
○
○
○

06 WEDNESDAY
○
○
○
○
○
○
○
○

07 THURSDAY
○
○
○
○
○
○
○
○

08 FRIDAY
○
○
○
○
○

May
2020

09 SATURDAY

○ _____
○ _____
○ _____
○ _____
○ _____
○ _____
○ _____
○ _____

10 SUNDAY

○ _____
○ _____
○ _____
○ _____
○ _____
○ _____
○ _____
○ _____

11 MONDAY

○ _____
○ _____
○ _____
○ _____
○ _____
○ _____
○ _____
○ _____

12 TUESDAY

○ _____
○ _____
○ _____
○ _____
○ _____

13 WEDNESDAY

○
○
○
○
○
○
○
○

14 THURSDAY

○
○
○
○
○
○
○
○

15 FRIDAY

○
○
○
○
○
○
○
○

16 SATURDAY

○
○
○
○
○

17 SUNDAY

○ _____
○ _____
○ _____
○ _____
○ _____
○ _____
○ _____
○ _____

18 MONDAY

○ _____
○ _____
○ _____
○ _____
○ _____
○ _____
○ _____
○ _____
○ _____

19 TUESDAY

○ _____
○ _____
○ _____
○ _____
○ _____
○ _____
○ _____
○ _____

20 WEDNESDAY

○ _____
○ _____
○ _____
○ _____
○ _____

May
2020

21 THURSDAY
○
○
○
○
○
○
○
○

22 FRIDAY
○
○
○
○
○
○
○
○

23 SATURDAY
○
○
○
○
○
○
○
○

24 SUNDAY
○
○
○
○
○

25 MONDAY

○ _____
○ _____
○ _____
○ _____
○ _____
○ _____
○ _____
○ _____

26 TUESDAY

○ _____
○ _____
○ _____
○ _____
○ _____
○ _____
○ _____
○ _____

27 WEDNESDAY

○ _____
○ _____
○ _____
○ _____
○ _____
○ _____
○ _____
○ _____

28 THURSDAY

○ _____
○ _____
○ _____
○ _____
○ _____

May
2020

29 FRIDAY
- ○
- ○
- ○
- ○
- ○
- ○
- ○
- ○

30 SATURDAY
- ○
- ○
- ○
- ○
- ○
- ○
- ○
- ○

31 SUNDAY
- ○
- ○
- ○
- ○
- ○
- ○
- ○
- ○

NOTES

June
2020

01 MONDAY
- ○ _____
- ○ _____
- ○ _____
- ○ _____
- ○ _____
- ○ _____
- ○ _____
- ○ _____

02 TUESDAY
- ○ _____
- ○ _____
- ○ _____
- ○ _____
- ○ _____
- ○ _____
- ○ _____
- ○ _____

03 WEDNESDAY
- ○ _____
- ○ _____
- ○ _____
- ○ _____
- ○ _____
- ○ _____
- ○ _____
- ○ _____

04 THURSDAY
- ○ _____
- ○ _____
- ○ _____
- ○ _____
- ○ _____

June
2020

05 FRIDAY

○ _____
○ _____
○ _____
○ _____
○ _____
○ _____
○ _____
○ _____

06 SATURDAY

○ _____
○ _____
○ _____
○ _____
○ _____
○ _____
○ _____
○ _____

07 SUNDAY

○ _____
○ _____
○ _____
○ _____
○ _____
○ _____
○ _____
○ _____

08 MONDAY

○ _____
○ _____
○ _____
○ _____
○ _____

09 TUESDAY

○ _____
○ _____
○ _____
○ _____
○ _____
○ _____
○ _____
○ _____

10 WEDNESDAY

○ _____
○ _____
○ _____
○ _____
○ _____
○ _____
○ _____
○ _____

11 THURSDAY

○ _____
○ _____
○ _____
○ _____
○ _____
○ _____
○ _____
○ _____

12 FRIDAY

○ _____
○ _____
○ _____
○ _____
○ _____

13 SATURDAY

○ _____
○ _____
○ _____
○ _____
○ _____
○ _____
○ _____
○ _____

14 SUNDAY

○ _____
○ _____
○ _____
○ _____
○ _____
○ _____
○ _____
○ _____

15 MONDAY

○ _____
○ _____
○ _____
○ _____
○ _____
○ _____
○ _____
○ _____

16 TUESDAY

○ _____
○ _____
○ _____
○ _____
○ _____

17 WEDNESDAY

○ _____
○ _____
○ _____
○ _____
○ _____
○ _____
○ _____
○ _____

18 THURSDAY

○ _____
○ _____
○ _____
○ _____
○ _____
○ _____
○ _____
○ _____

19 FRIDAY

○ _____
○ _____
○ _____
○ _____
○ _____
○ _____
○ _____
○ _____

20 SATURDAY

○ _____
○ _____
○ _____
○ _____
○ _____

June
2020

21 SUNDAY

○ _____
○ _____
○ _____
○ _____
○ _____
○ _____
○ _____
○ _____

22 MONDAY

○ _____
○ _____
○ _____
○ _____
○ _____
○ _____
○ _____
○ _____

23 TUESDAY

○ _____
○ _____
○ _____
○ _____
○ _____
○ _____
○ _____
○ _____

24 WEDNESDAY

○ _____
○ _____
○ _____
○ _____
○ _____

25 THURSDAY
- ○
- ○
- ○
- ○
- ○
- ○
- ○
- ○

26 FRIDAY
- ○
- ○
- ○
- ○
- ○
- ○
- ○
- ○

27 SATURDAY
- ○
- ○
- ○
- ○
- ○
- ○
- ○
- ○

28 SUNDAY
- ○
- ○
- ○
- ○
- ○

June
2020

29 MONDAY

○ _____
○ _____
○ _____
○ _____
○ _____
○ _____
○ _____
○ _____

30 TUESDAY

○ _____
○ _____
○ _____
○ _____
○ _____
○ _____
○ _____
○ _____

NOTES

_____
_____
_____
_____
_____
_____
_____
_____
_____
_____
_____
_____

July
2020

01 WEDNESDAY

○ _____
○ _____
○ _____
○ _____
○ _____
○ _____
○ _____

02 THURSDAY

○ _____
○ _____
○ _____
○ _____
○ _____
○ _____
○ _____
○ _____

03 FRIDAY

○ _____
○ _____
○ _____
○ _____
○ _____
○ _____
○ _____
○ _____

04 SATURDAY

○ _____
○ _____
○ _____
○ _____
○ _____

05 SUNDAY

○ _____
○ _____
○ _____
○ _____
○ _____
○ _____
○ _____
○ _____

06 MONDAY

○ _____
○ _____
○ _____
○ _____
○ _____
○ _____
○ _____
○ _____
○ _____

07 TUESDAY

○ _____
○ _____
○ _____
○ _____
○ _____
○ _____
○ _____
○ _____

08 WEDNESDAY

○ _____
○ _____
○ _____
○ _____
○ _____

09 THURSDAY
○
○
○
○
○
○
○

10 FRIDAY
○
○
○
○
○
○
○
○

11 SATURDAY
○
○
○
○
○
○
○
○

12 SUNDAY
○
○
○
○
○

13 MONDAY

○
○
○
○
○
○
○
○

14 TUESDAY

○
○
○
○
○
○
○
○

15 WEDNESDAY

○
○
○
○
○
○
○
○

16 THURSDAY

○
○
○
○
○

July

2020

17 FRIDAY

○
○
○
○
○
○
○
○

18 SATURDAY

○
○
○
○
○
○
○
○

19 SUNDAY

○
○
○
○
○
○
○
○

20 MONDAY

○
○
○
○
○

July

2020

21 TUESDAY

○

○

○

○

○

○

○

○

22 WEDNESDAY

○

○

○

○

○

○

○

○

○

23 THURSDAY

○

○

○

○

○

○

○

○

24 FRIDAY

○

○

○

○

○

25 SATURDAY

○ _____
○ _____
○ _____
○ _____
○ _____
○ _____
○ _____
○ _____

26 SUNDAY

○ _____
○ _____
○ _____
○ _____
○ _____
○ _____
○ _____
○ _____

27 MONDAY

○ _____
○ _____
○ _____
○ _____
○ _____
○ _____
○ _____
○ _____

28 TUESDAY

○ _____
○ _____
○ _____
○ _____
○ _____

29 WEDNESDAY

- ○ _____
- ○ _____
- ○ _____
- ○ _____
- ○ _____
- ○ _____
- ○ _____
- ○ _____

30 THURSDAY

- ○ _____
- ○ _____
- ○ _____
- ○ _____
- ○ _____
- ○ _____
- ○ _____
- ○ _____

31 FRIDAY

- ○ _____
- ○ _____
- ○ _____
- ○ _____
- ○ _____
- ○ _____
- ○ _____
- ○ _____

NOTES

_____
_____
_____
_____

August
2020

01 SATURDAY

○ _____
○ _____
○ _____
○ _____
○ _____
○ _____
○ _____
○ _____

02 SUNDAY

○ _____
○ _____
○ _____
○ _____
○ _____
○ _____
○ _____
○ _____

03 MONDAY

○ _____
○ _____
○ _____
○ _____
○ _____
○ _____
○ _____
○ _____

04 TUESDAY

○ _____
○ _____
○ _____
○ _____
○ _____

August
2020

05 WEDNESDAY

○ _____
○ _____
○ _____
○ _____
○ _____
○ _____
○ _____
○ _____

06 THURSDAY

○ _____
○ _____
○ _____
○ _____
○ _____
○ _____
○ _____
○ _____

07 FRIDAY

○ _____
○ _____
○ _____
○ _____
○ _____
○ _____
○ _____
○ _____

08 SATURDAY

○ _____
○ _____
○ _____
○ _____
○ _____

09 SUNDAY

○ _____
○ _____
○ _____
○ _____
○ _____
○ _____
○ _____
○ _____

10 MONDAY

○ _____
○ _____
○ _____
○ _____
○ _____
○ _____
○ _____
○ _____

11 TUESDAY

○ _____
○ _____
○ _____
○ _____
○ _____
○ _____
○ _____
○ _____

12 WEDNESDAY

○ _____
○ _____
○ _____
○ _____
○ _____

13 THURSDAY

○ _____
○ _____
○ _____
○ _____
○ _____
○ _____
○ _____
○ _____

14 FRIDAY

○ _____
○ _____
○ _____
○ _____
○ _____
○ _____
○ _____
○ _____

15 SATURDAY

○ _____
○ _____
○ _____
○ _____
○ _____
○ _____
○ _____
○ _____

16 SUNDAY

○ _____
○ _____
○ _____
○ _____
○ _____

17 MONDAY

○
○
○
○
○
○
○

18 TUESDAY

○
○
○
○
○
○
○
○

19 WEDNESDAY

○
○
○
○
○
○
○
○

20 THURSDAY

○
○
○
○
○

21 FRIDAY

○ _____
○ _____
○ _____
○ _____
○ _____
○ _____
○ _____
○ _____

22 SATURDAY

○ _____
○ _____
○ _____
○ _____
○ _____
○ _____
○ _____
○ _____

23 SUNDAY

○ _____
○ _____
○ _____
○ _____
○ _____
○ _____
○ _____
○ _____

24 MONDAY

○ _____
○ _____
○ _____
○ _____
○ _____

25 TUESDAY

○ _____
○ _____
○ _____
○ _____
○ _____
○ _____
○ _____
○ _____

26 WEDNESDAY

○ _____
○ _____
○ _____
○ _____
○ _____
○ _____
○ _____
○ _____

27 THURSDAY

○ _____
○ _____
○ _____
○ _____
○ _____
○ _____
○ _____
○ _____

28 FRIDAY

○ _____
○ _____
○ _____
○ _____
○ _____

August
2020

29 SATURDAY

○ _____
○ _____
○ _____
○ _____
○ _____
○ _____
○ _____
○ _____

30 SUNDAY

○ _____
○ _____
○ _____
○ _____
○ _____
○ _____
○ _____
○ _____

31 MONDAY

○ _____
○ _____
○ _____
○ _____
○ _____
○ _____
○ _____
○ _____

NOTES

_____
_____
_____
_____

01 TUESDAY

○ _____
○ _____
○ _____
○ _____
○ _____
○ _____
○ _____
○ _____

02 WEDNESDAY

○ _____
○ _____
○ _____
○ _____
○ _____
○ _____
○ _____
○ _____

03 THURSDAY

○ _____
○ _____
○ _____
○ _____
○ _____
○ _____
○ _____
○ _____

04 FRIDAY

○ _____
○ _____
○ _____
○ _____
○ _____

September
2020

05 SATURDAY

○ _____
○ _____
○ _____
○ _____
○ _____
○ _____
○ _____
○ _____

06 SUNDAY

○ _____
○ _____
○ _____
○ _____
○ _____
○ _____
○ _____
○ _____

07 MONDAY

○ _____
○ _____
○ _____
○ _____
○ _____
○ _____
○ _____
○ _____

08 TUESDAY

○ _____
○ _____
○ _____
○ _____
○ _____

09 WEDNESDAY

○ _____
○ _____
○ _____
○ _____
○ _____
○ _____
○ _____
○ _____

10 THURSDAY

○ _____
○ _____
○ _____
○ _____
○ _____
○ _____
○ _____
○ _____

11 FRIDAY

○ _____
○ _____
○ _____
○ _____
○ _____
○ _____
○ _____
○ _____

12 SATURDAY

○ _____
○ _____
○ _____
○ _____
○ _____

13 SUNDAY

○
○
○
○
○
○
○
○

14 MONDAY

○
○
○
○
○
○
○
○

15 TUESDAY

○
○
○
○
○
○
○
○

16 WEDNESDAY

○
○
○
○
○

17 THURSDAY

○ _____
○ _____
○ _____
○ _____
○ _____
○ _____
○ _____
○ _____

18 FRIDAY

○ _____
○ _____
○ _____
○ _____
○ _____
○ _____
○ _____
○ _____

19 SATURDAY

○ _____
○ _____
○ _____
○ _____
○ _____
○ _____
○ _____
○ _____

20 SUNDAY

○ _____
○ _____
○ _____
○ _____
○ _____

21 MONDAY

○
○
○
○
○
○
○
○

22 TUESDAY

○
○
○
○
○
○
○
○

23 WEDNESDAY

○
○
○
○
○
○
○
○

24 THURSDAY

○
○
○
○
○

25 FRIDAY

○ _____
○ _____
○ _____
○ _____
○ _____
○ _____
○ _____
○ _____

26 SATURDAY

○ _____
○ _____
○ _____
○ _____
○ _____
○ _____
○ _____
○ _____

27 SUNDAY

○ _____
○ _____
○ _____
○ _____
○ _____
○ _____
○ _____
○ _____

28 MONDAY

○ _____
○ _____
○ _____
○ _____
○ _____

29 TUESDAY

○ _____
○ _____
○ _____
○ _____
○ _____
○ _____
○ _____
○ _____

30 WEDNESDAY

○ _____
○ _____
○ _____
○ _____
○ _____
○ _____
○ _____
○ _____

NOTES

_____
_____
_____
_____
_____
_____
_____
_____
_____
_____
_____
_____
_____

October
2020

01 THURSDAY

○
○
○
○
○
○
○

02 FRIDAY

○
○
○
○
○
○
○
○

03 SATURDAY

○
○
○
○
○
○
○
○

04 SUNDAY

○
○
○
○
○

05 MONDAY

○
○
○
○
○
○
○
○

06 TUESDAY

○
○
○
○
○
○
○
○

07 WEDNESDAY

○
○
○
○
○
○
○
○

08 THURSDAY

○
○
○
○
○

09 FRIDAY

○ _____
○ _____
○ _____
○ _____
○ _____
○ _____
○ _____
○ _____

10 SATURDAY

○ _____
○ _____
○ _____
○ _____
○ _____
○ _____
○ _____
○ _____

11 SUNDAY

○ _____
○ _____
○ _____
○ _____
○ _____
○ _____
○ _____
○ _____

12 MONDAY

○ _____
○ _____
○ _____
○ _____
○ _____

13 TUESDAY

○ _____
○ _____
○ _____
○ _____
○ _____
○ _____
○ _____
○ _____

14 WEDNESDAY

○ _____
○ _____
○ _____
○ _____
○ _____
○ _____
○ _____
○ _____

15 THURSDAY

○ _____
○ _____
○ _____
○ _____
○ _____
○ _____
○ _____
○ _____

16 FRIDAY

○ _____
○ _____
○ _____
○ _____
○ _____

17 SATURDAY

○
○
○
○
○
○
○
○

18 SUNDAY

○
○
○
○
○
○
○
○

19 MONDAY

○
○
○
○
○
○
○
○

20 TUESDAY

○
○
○
○
○

21 WEDNESDAY
○
○
○
○
○
○
○
○

22 THURSDAY
○
○
○
○
○
○
○
○

23 FRIDAY
○
○
○
○
○
○
○
○

24 SATURDAY
○
○
○
○
○

25 SUNDAY

○ _____
○ _____
○ _____
○ _____
○ _____
○ _____
○ _____
○ _____

26 MONDAY

○ _____
○ _____
○ _____
○ _____
○ _____
○ _____
○ _____
○ _____

27 TUESDAY

○ _____
○ _____
○ _____
○ _____
○ _____
○ _____
○ _____
○ _____

28 WEDNESDAY

○ _____
○ _____
○ _____
○ _____
○ _____

29 THURSDAY

○
○
○
○
○
○
○
○

30 FRIDAY

○
○
○
○
○
○
○
○
○

31 SATURDAY

○
○
○
○
○
○
○
○

NOTES

November
2020

01 SUNDAY

○ _____
○ _____
○ _____
○ _____
○ _____
○ _____
○ _____
○ _____

02 MONDAY

○ _____
○ _____
○ _____
○ _____
○ _____
○ _____
○ _____
○ _____

03 TUESDAY

○ _____
○ _____
○ _____
○ _____
○ _____
○ _____
○ _____
○ _____

04 WEDNESDAY

○ _____
○ _____
○ _____
○ _____
○ _____

05 THURSDAY

○ _____
○ _____
○ _____
○ _____
○ _____
○ _____
○ _____
○ _____

06 FRIDAY

○ _____
○ _____
○ _____
○ _____
○ _____
○ _____
○ _____
○ _____

07 SATURDAY

○ _____
○ _____
○ _____
○ _____
○ _____
○ _____
○ _____
○ _____

08 SUNDAY

○ _____
○ _____
○ _____
○ _____
○ _____

09 MONDAY

○ _____
○ _____
○ _____
○ _____
○ _____
○ _____
○ _____
○ _____

10 TUESDAY

○ _____
○ _____
○ _____
○ _____
○ _____
○ _____
○ _____
○ _____

11 WEDNESDAY

○ _____
○ _____
○ _____
○ _____
○ _____
○ _____
○ _____
○ _____

12 THURSDAY

○ _____
○ _____
○ _____
○ _____
○ _____

November
2020

13 FRIDAY

○ _____
○ _____
○ _____
○ _____
○ _____
○ _____
○ _____
○ _____

14 SATURDAY

○ _____
○ _____
○ _____
○ _____
○ _____
○ _____
○ _____
○ _____

15 SUNDAY

○ _____
○ _____
○ _____
○ _____
○ _____
○ _____
○ _____
○ _____

16 MONDAY

○ _____
○ _____
○ _____
○ _____
○ _____

17 TUESDAY

○ _____
○ _____
○ _____
○ _____
○ _____
○ _____
○ _____
○ _____

18 WEDNESDAY

○ _____
○ _____
○ _____
○ _____
○ _____
○ _____
○ _____
○ _____

19 THURSDAY

○ _____
○ _____
○ _____
○ _____
○ _____
○ _____
○ _____
○ _____

20 FRIDAY

○ _____
○ _____
○ _____
○ _____
○ _____

November
2020

21 SATURDAY

○
○
○
○
○
○
○
○

22 SUNDAY

○
○
○
○
○
○
○
○

23 MONDAY

○
○
○
○
○
○
○
○

24 TUESDAY

○
○
○
○
○

25 WEDNESDAY
○
○
○
○
○
○
○
○

26 THURSDAY
○
○
○
○
○
○
○
○
○

27 FRIDAY
○
○
○
○
○
○
○
○

28 SATURDAY
○
○
○
○
○

November
2020

29 SUNDAY

○ _____
○ _____
○ _____
○ _____
○ _____
○ _____
○ _____
○ _____

30 MONDAY

○ _____
○ _____
○ _____
○ _____
○ _____
○ _____
○ _____
○ _____

NOTES

_____
_____
_____
_____
_____
_____
_____
_____
_____
_____
_____
_____
_____

December
2020

01 TUESDAY

○ _____
○ _____
○ _____
○ _____
○ _____
○ _____
○ _____
○ _____

02 WEDNESDAY

○ _____
○ _____
○ _____
○ _____
○ _____
○ _____
○ _____
○ _____

03 THURSDAY

○ _____
○ _____
○ _____
○ _____
○ _____
○ _____
○ _____
○ _____

04 FRIDAY

○ _____
○ _____
○ _____
○ _____
○ _____

December
2020

05 SATURDAY

○
○
○
○
○
○
○
○

06 SUNDAY

○
○
○
○
○
○
○
○

07 MONDAY

○
○
○
○
○
○
○
○

08 TUESDAY

○
○
○
○
○

December
2020

09 WEDNESDAY

10 THURSDAY

11 FRIDAY

12 SATURDAY

December
2020

13 SUNDAY
- ○
- ○
- ○
- ○
- ○
- ○
- ○
- ○

14 MONDAY
- ○
- ○
- ○
- ○
- ○
- ○
- ○
- ○

15 TUESDAY
- ○
- ○
- ○
- ○
- ○
- ○
- ○
- ○

16 WEDNESDAY
- ○
- ○
- ○
- ○
- ○

17 THURSDAY

○
○
○
○
○
○
○
○

18 FRIDAY

○
○
○
○
○
○
○
○

19 SATURDAY

○
○
○
○
○
○
○
○

20 SUNDAY

○
○
○
○
○

December
2020

21 MONDAY

○
○
○
○
○
○
○
○

22 TUESDAY

○
○
○
○
○
○
○
○

23 WEDNESDAY

○
○
○
○
○
○
○
○

24 THURSDAY

○
○
○
○
○

25 FRIDAY

○ _____
○ _____
○ _____
○ _____
○ _____
○ _____
○ _____
○ _____

26 SATURDAY

○ _____
○ _____
○ _____
○ _____
○ _____
○ _____
○ _____
○ _____

27 SUNDAY

○ _____
○ _____
○ _____
○ _____
○ _____
○ _____
○ _____
○ _____

28 MONDAY

○ _____
○ _____
○ _____
○ _____
○ _____

December

2020

29 TUESDAY

○ _____
○ _____
○ _____
○ _____
○ _____
○ _____
○ _____
○ _____

30 WEDNESDAY

○ _____
○ _____
○ _____
○ _____
○ _____
○ _____
○ _____
○ _____

31 THURSDAY

○ _____
○ _____
○ _____
○ _____
○ _____
○ _____
○ _____
○ _____

NOTES

_____
_____
_____
_____

Made in the USA
Coppell, TX
22 December 2019